Without Goodbyes

From Puritan Deerfield to Mohawk Kahnawake

Without Goodbyes

From Puritan Deerfield to Mohawk Kahnawake

Poems by Ginny Lowe Connors

Turning Point

Published by Turning Point
P.O. Box 541106
Cincinnati, OH 45254-1106

ISBN: 9781625493965

Poetry Editor: Kevin Walzer
Business Editor: Lori Jareo

Cover Design: Cindy Stewart
Cover Art: Virginia Dehn

Acknowledgments

Freshwater Literary Journal: "Everything She Knows Goes Up in Smoke," "Thirty Miles the First Day," "They Eat. They Sleep."

Thanks also to David Bosse of the Deerfield Memorial Library for his helpful sharing of research materials.

Many thanks to Dwayne Stacey for guiding me through present-day Kahnawake and sharing valuable information.

I appreciate the valuable input from those who have read early drafts of some of these poems, especially Christine Beck, Sherri Bedingfield, Debbie Gilbert, Pat Hale, Joan Hofmann, Nancy Kerrigan, Julia Paul, and Elaine Zimmerman. Also appreciated are Leslie Ullman and Wyn Cooper for their very helpful suggestions.

Thank you, Marty, for accompanying me on research trips and listening to me talk about this project.

Thank you, Cindy Stewart, for your help formatting the manuscript.

Table of Contents

Introduction

This collection of poems is a work of imagination based on a historical event: the infamous 1704 raid on the village of Deerfield, Massachusetts. The raid took place during a harsh winter, when piles of snow leaned against the palisade that surrounded much of the village, making it easy for raiders to climb up the snowbanks and leap into the fortified town just before dawn. Over 200 Mohawk and Huron warriors, along with about 40 French troops carried out the raid. Each group had its own reasons for participating in the attack on Deerfield. The First Nations warriors primarily wanted to take captives. The French soldiers wanted to earn recognition for their prowess, and so advance in the ranks. The Governor-General of New France, Philippe de Rigaud de Vaudreuil, wished to consolidate his alliance with the Native groups.

Many were killed. Some escaped. More than 100 Deerfield residents: men, women, and children, were captured. Then they began the 300-mile trek to New France, the French colony, in Quebec.

The poems here focus on Joanna Kellogg, an eleven-year-old girl, and two of her siblings, Joseph and Rebecca. They were adopted into Mohawk families in the village of Kahnawake, a Mohawk community centered around a Jesuit mission. Most of the families there were nominally Catholic, although they continued their Native traditions and beliefs. Several of the young Deerfield captives were brought to Kahnawake; others went to different places near or in Montreal.

The Mohawks, or People of the Flint, as they preferred to be called, did not have a written language at that time, but they had a rich culture with a way of life that offered more freedom than the Puritan lifestyle, and that also offered considerably more power to women. It was a matrilineal society, and child-rearing practices were lenient and kind. Young captives often adapted very well. Older captives were most often held for ransom, as they did not adapt so easily.

For me, history is best understood through a look at the individuals involved, and how their lives changed as a result of the upheavals of history. Poetry is a way to get at emotional truths, and those are truths that matter to me. Truths? Most of the story presented here is imagined. While it does not conflict with historical accounts, records about the Mohawks in this time period are scanty. This collection of poems is my attempt to understand what it may have been like to be thrust suddenly into a completely different culture, and ultimately to adapt and thrive. The physical journey Joanna took to reach Kahnawake must have been grueling; the journey she took to truly become a member of the Mohawk community there is the bigger story.

North America is composed of many such stories, as we are a society made up of people who are descended from First Nations people, slaves, indentured servants, and immigrants. The ability to adapt to change is crucial to survival. It's interesting to consider individual tales of how that is accomplished. It's in that spirit that these poems are presented.

Directory of Names

For the purposes of this book, real people are included alongside fictional characters. Some documentation on the people from Deerfield exists, but little is known about specific First Nation individuals who lived in Kahnawake in the early 1700s.

The Kellogg family
Martin Kellogg Sr.: Taken prisoner, ransomed and returned to Massachusetts in 1706.

Sarah Dickinson Lane Kellogg: Second wife of Martin. Escaped during the raid.

Martin Kellogg Jr.: Son of Martin Sr. and his first wife, he was about seventeen years old when captured and brought to Sault-au-Recollect.

Joseph Kellogg: Aged twelve when captured, he stayed at Kahnawake until adulthood. In this book, at Kahnawakhe, he is called Spotted Colt.

Joanna Kellogg: She was eleven at the time of the raid. She married and raised children in Kahnawake, and lived there for most of her life. In this book, at Kahnawake, she is called Ohne-kanos-iaote or White Feather.

Rebecca Kellogg: She was eight at the time of the raid. She grew up at Kahnawakhe, married and raised a family there. In this book, Joanna refers to her as Becca until they become accustomed to Kahnawakhe, where she is called Little Bird.

Jonathan Kellogg: Killed in the raid. He was five years old.

The Burt Family
Benjamin Burt: A young man married to Sarah.

Sarah Burt: Heavily pregnant during the time of the raid, she managed the trek to Canada and gave birth to a boy shortly after arrival.

Christopher Burt: Firstborn son of Benjamin and Sarah Burt

The Williams Family
Reverend John Williams: The most prominent member of the Deerfield community. On arrival in New France, he and three of his children: Esther, Samuel, and Warham, were turned over to French authorities in or near Montreal and held there until they were ransomed in 1706.

(Mrs.) Eunice Williams: The wife of Reverend Williams, she died during the trek to Canada.

Eunice Williams: Age seven when the raid took place, Eunice was adopted by a Mohawk family who had lost their child to smallpox. She stayed at Kahnawake for the rest of her life. In this book, at Kahnawakhe, she is called She-Is-Planted.

Father Jacques Bruyas: He was a Jesuit missionary who worked with the Onondagas, the Hurons, and the Mohawks, often urging warring groups to negotiate for peace. He was active at the Kahnawake mission.

Kateri Tekakwitha: Informally known as the Lily of the Mohawks, and now known as Saint Kateri Tekakwitha, she survived smallpox but her face was seriously scarred. She converted to Catholicism and was known for her virtue and religiosity. At her death in Kahnawake at the age of 24, witnesses said that her scars vanished and her face glowed radiantly. Various miracles are attributed to her. She died about two decades before the Deerfield captives arrived at Kahnawake, but was still spoken of reverently.

Some Deerfield Captives
Mercy Carter: Ten years old at time of the raid, she remained in Kahnawake for life.

<u>Elizabeth Hull</u>: Sixteen years old at the time of the attack, brought to Kahnawake but later redeemed.

<u>Billy (William) Brooks</u>: Captured at age six, never returned to the colonies.

John Sheldon: His wife was killed during the Deerfield raid and several of his children were captured, but he was not home that night. He traveled to Canada several times and negotiated for the release of certain Deerfield captives.

Mehitable Nims: Killed during the Deerfield raid. She was seven years old.

The names of the Mohawks of Kahnawake in the 1700s are unavailable. For this reason, the names used in this book are imagined by the author.

Joanna's Kahnawake Family:
<u>Red Leaf</u>: Joanna's adoptive mother. A widow, she is the sister of Stands-in-Shadow.

<u>Stands-in-Shadow</u>: Becca's adoptive mother, wife of Splits-the-Sky.

<u>Teka-ron-hioken or Splits-the-Sky</u>: Takes charge of the Kellogg sisters during the raid; he is the husband of Stands-in-Shadow.

<u>Big Grandmother</u>: The mother of Red Leaf and Stands-in-Shadow.

Some Young Men of Kahnawake: <u>Young Otter</u>, <u>Cold Moon</u>, <u>Throws-Many-Stones</u>, <u>Dragging Canoe</u>

Some Young Women of Kahnawake: <u>Following Spring</u>, <u>Long Neck</u>, <u>Makes-the-Grass-Wave</u>,

Some Girls of Kahnawake: <u>Moonface</u>, <u>Twig</u>, <u>Gray Dawn</u>

Others

Skywatcher: a respected shaman

Three Deer: Joseph's adoptive father

Cloud Woman: Young Otter's great-grandmother

Bernadette: Young woman who works for priests at the mission, preparing meals and cleaning

Standing Elk: Red Leaf's deceased husband

1704-1706

Everything She Knows Goes Up in Smoke

Deerfield Village, Massachusetts, February 29, 1704

The night before, her hands chapped and stupid,
Joanna dropped a redware pitcher,
watched it shatter. Her mother's flare of anger!
Sudden sting of a slap. Her father's pinched lips.

And now this broken morning,
how red the rising sun.
The air so cold, already her heart is freezing.
The wind shrieks
and a pig too, galloping past them,
a hatchet in its side, a savage chasing after it
and a French soldier laughing like the very devil.

Blood on the snow.
Bodies. Mash of footprints everywhere.
A woman's shawl whipping in the wind—
some crippled thing trying to fly.
Flames roaring, consuming their homes.
Thick curdles of smoke.
Its acrid smell mixes with the odor of blood,
cold sweat. Can this be real?

Survivors herded toward the meeting house,
she among them. The men are roped like calves.
Where is her father? There's Joseph, his face all smudged.
Becca clutches her hand, nose running, eyes
like pewter plates.

Raiders strut   push   shout
in words she doesn't know, hauling away
woolens and kettles, bread and bacon.
And prisoners—a hundred Deerfield villagers,
many of them children, like Joanna.

Reverend Williams, their leading citizen,
moves meekly along, his eyes tearing, lips sputtering.

She tries not to cry, but cinders lodge in her eye.
Crows flap and hop among the slaughtered,
repeating Ack! Ack! Ack!

Joanna pulls her sister along, but turns
to look back, and sees a figure in nightclothes fleeing
toward the woods—her mother
abandoning them, abandoning them.

Thirty Miles the First Day

Hills, branches, shards of ice, feet of ice.
Fingers red and cracking. Place your feet
into the footsteps of those who've gone before.
The old life—hacked away. Up in flames.
Your job now is to survive.
Faster, go faster. If you must cry, cry silently.

      Keep moving, keep moving.

A baby that cries too much
is killed. And a girl who falls into drifts
and flounders, complains, sobs
I can't, I can't.
Killed.

      Keep moving, keep moving.

Faster, faster. Becca struggles to keep up.
Where is Mama she asks, *where is Mama?*
Joanna doesn't answer, just pulls her along.
She's swallowed a rock. It's lodged in her throat.
Her stomach twists in on itself. A few sinewy Indians
run along their ranks scowling, grunting,
tugging, pushing. They must go faster.

Do not think.
Fill the mind with blankness
like endless snow, like pale dull sky.

      Keep moving, keep moving.

Crossing Green River

The river is not green, but black,
and rushing swiftly, ice clutching its shoreline,
chunks of frozen snow barreling down the waterway,
pine branches covered with white
stretching bony fingers over the water.

And the river is not wide, but treacherous.
Clotted with ice, it rushes, it roils
and they are made to cross it.

Goodwife Williams is not able—she loses
her balance and is swept away downriver,
and when she's dragged ashore, a heavy burden
in her wet clothes, she's choking and spitting,
shuddering and moaning, refusing
to get up, so they tomahawk her, and the reverend
near-faints, but Joanna's own father sets
his mouth to firm and crosses the river,
getting wet to his thighs.
Joanna hangs back.

And the smallest children are not able
so their Indian masters carry them across—
they have masters, they are prisoners now—
while the Deerfield men and oldest boys
splash through the rushing water and some bad words
are shouted out and an owl startles off
into the frigid afternoon woods.
And Joanna hangs back.

Finally, seeing she is not able to make herself
cross over, Martin, her big, strong half-brother, comes back
across for Joanna, and she notices how red his nose is,
and his cheeks, from sunburn or windburn or just the cold,

she doesn't know, and his trousers are torn and damp,
but he holds her arm firmly and helps her plunge through
the freezing channel and climb over sharp rocks that hide
beneath the water and litter the shoreline.

Joanna's feet seem not part of her body
but strange, unfeeling objects, whitish-yellow
pieces of wood, scraped and useless, but the rest of her
stings like a thousand sewing needles and the skirts
tied up upon crossing have been splashed, they are
stiffening with ice and her teeth clack-clack-clack.

She wants to lie down right there, but they are not
allowed to rest, she wants to run into a field of snow,
silent and silvery beneath the sky, and lie down forever
but they are made to jump and slap themselves,
to get the blood moving, her brother says, and on they go
a few miles more till they come to the hidden stash.

It's not visible at first, but they hear dogs whining
and when pine branches are dragged away from the opening
of a shallow cave, they find several crude sleds
and dogs to pull them, animal furs, strips of dried meat and fruit,
and best of all, Indian shoes that lace up to the knees
and are soft, are warm.

And something else unfamiliar to the captives—
those curious paddle-like contraptions the Indians use
where snow is deep: *snowshoes.*

Three wounded warriors will not have to be carried anymore,
they're helped into the sleds, along with
the youngest children and the heaviest packs.

And they go on.

They Eat. They Sleep.

The French soldiers have left them. The Indians—
Mohawks mostly—some Hurons, and the captives
toil on. Hard travel for   days?   weeks?   months?
and then they rest two days in a row. A fire is allowed.
Joanna must gather twigs and branches to feed it.

In the flames she sees her home burning. Billowing smoke.
The screams. But she is cold. She is hungry.
She folds the past carefully away.
The burning wood spits and snaps. Sparks
spiral into the darkening sky. Where do they go?

Where are we going? Becca asks.
        To the Indians' place.
When will we get there?
        Joanna doesn't answer. Because...and then? What?
Slams those questions away.

Dizzy for a minute. It's the scent of roasting meat.
Some men have killed a moose. The edges of a big
skewered hunk turn crisp. Fat sizzles in the embers.
That night they feast. Moose meat, dried cranberries,
ground nuts. She gets her fair share.

Joseph sits near them as they eat, his lips greasy,
his freckled face streaked with dirt, his dark hair a thicket.
Only his eyes shine, excited by the hunt. Says he'll be
a great hunter himself someday. Says farming
is terrible dull. Oh, that boy always was a little wild.

For the first time, Joanna sleeps through the night
even as a chill seeps through the pine branches,
her makeshift mattress. Teka-ron-hioken,
her master, has a long scar that splits his cheek,

22

but he's not all bad. He's given the sisters a robe of animal fur.
They sleep surrounded by Indians and ragged neighbors.
Snores, groans. A quick yelp. And off in the woods, coyotes
yip, bark, howl. The sled dogs answer. Joanna shuts it all out,
falls heavily into dreams— the white chicken that would
follow her, a skein of yellow yarn unraveling—dreams
she won't remember on waking.

The Strong and the Beautiful

If Joanna ever marries, it will be to a man like Ben,
Sarah Burt's young husband. Secretly, Joanna admires

his dark curly hair, his straight white teeth. He's
thoughtful, mature. That deep crease between his eyes.

He wraps an arm around his wife, who cradles her belly,
round as a melon. Sarah pants when the walking gets hard.

Whew, whew, whew. But never complains. Ben rakes
his hand through his hair, murmurs something to his wife

and Joanna watches her pause. Eyes bright, her voice flares—
We will survive this journey! And our child will live.

*He will grow up brave and strong. Ben, you believe it…
don't you?*   Yes, yes, of course, Ben Burt agrees,

although his expression is dazed, uncertain.
Joanna can't help asking: *What if your child is a girl?*

Sarah turns to her. The woman's cheeks are mottled,
her lips chapped. A twig is caught in her tangled hair.

But her voice is firm and clear.
Even a girl can be brave, can be strong.

Parted

Six Indians and a handful of captives leave that morning
and do not return. Afternoon, a dozen others
go off a different way. All day Joanna watches

a quiet snow filling in their footprints.
And then her father comes to say good-bye.
He and Martin are to go with one group,

while Joanna, Becca, and Joseph will continue
with Teka-ron-hioken and some others.
Their father, distant and voiceless for days,

a sleepwalker staring at his feet, looks tighter
in his skin. Sharp. Aware. He hugs the three of them
one by one, looks into Joseph's eyes, then Joanna's, Becca's.

Do what they say, he tells them
as Becca clings to his leg. *Be brave. Don't forget
your English. Say your prayers. Don't forget…*

  But I thought we'd stay together! Joanna
protests. *I thought*—she cannot finish.
A redskin is gesturing at her father, saying *Go! Go!*

and another pulls Becca away.
  Will we see each other again?
Joanna tears the words from her throat, flings them

after her father and her half-brother. Martin
turns toward her and calls, *We will, we will!
We'll come for you! Don't forget us!*

and then they are gone. Joanna tries not to cry.
Their captors do not like crying

but her tears don't care, don't care at all—
they keep on falling. An Indian woman, one of two
who travels with them, puts her arms around Becca
and gives her a thin, hard stick of dried meat.

Becca throws it on the ground and yells, *I hate you!*
I hate you all! You killed my little brother!
You burned our house! You—

Teka-ron-hioken scoops her up and puts her
on a sled with Eunice Williams and the little Warner boy.
She digs her hands into her eyes, hiccups.

Joseph picks up the meat and chews on it,
says nothing, just stares and stares
in the direction their father has gone.

A Coating of Ice

They slept in shelters made of log poles and skins
as freezing rain clink-clinked against the hides.
But today the sun is a bright coin tossed high and far.
All the trees wear an armor of ice. Joanna blinks,
half-blind in all this light. Her thoughts are heavy
and black, though today the whole world shines.
It stretches out before her—

trees and snow, ice glitter. Questions
without answers, an emptiness coated in ice.

She is no place. She is no one. Joanna Kellogg
of Deerfield, brown-haired girl whose home
had a fine red door, whose mother taught her
the things a girl must know, whose father hummed
and worked his fields, brought her outside
to smell the turned soil, measure the height
of their corn—that girl's lost as a dream at dawn.

And her chickens with their warm eggs—
they're a story one tells little children.

She's been given a new name: Ohne-kanos-iaote.
Joseph, who talks to Indians as if he's forgotten
he's a white boy with a civilized tongue—
Joseph says he thinks the name means
White Feather. What kind of fool name is that?

Ohne-kanos-iaote?
No. That girl Joanna? No.
She is a stomach clenching.

They have run out of food.

They See a White Owl

Snow turns to slush. They keep going.
Joseph, who used to run back and forth,
talking, pointing, strutting—he's slowed down.

Rivers to cross, mountains to climb. Keep going.
At dusk a snowy owl glides overhead, a vision,
a ghost, a spirit leading them on. They all pause,

gaze upward. Something shifts inside Joanna.
To be in this wild place with the wind
carrying its pine scent, the moon rising,

all notion of chores erased—it's not entirely bad.
But the meat of two rabbits and a handful of beans
make a thin stew. Children are given their portions first

but never enough. As darkness settles over them,
Becca huddles against her sister, and Joanna feels the jut
of her small shoulder blades, sharp as plough blades.

Joanna and her sister are girls dressed in rags
who must stumble through a wilderness. If they could fly
above it all, wearing white feathers—but no.

A red star throbs on the horizon
and the night feels large around them.

Hills Go on Forever

Becca complains she is tired of this journey.
Are we almost there? she asks Joanna.

The hills go on forever. The rivers
go on forever. The sky.

> *No,* Joanna wants to say, but does not,
> *we will just keep walking, forever and ever.*

Some things do not last forever.
The screams in her head from that terrible day,

they're fading just a little. Now they're just wind—
a keening wind in her mind. And the soft white mounds

of snow don't last forever—already they're turning
to shrouds of fog as the days turn warmer.

And what does she recall of her mother? Her green eyes,
her quick, nervous hands. Her fleeing figure,

a phantom in nightclothes, pale against the snow.
She ran away. Her mother did, she ran away.

Terrified, as they'd all been. But for the captured,
for Joanna, too much fear, too much grief

was forbidden. The redskins tomahawked those
who were noisy in grief, those who were weak.

I said, are we almost there? Becca nags. A fly
buzzing in her ear, the girl's everlasting questions.

Joanna wonders what **there** could be. That faraway

place. Will they become slaves to the Indians?
Will they—*Are we almost—*

   Yes, snaps Joanna. *We're almost there.*

Spirit Calls at Lake Champlain

Near dusk, they make camp near a long lake.
In the day's last light, Joanna watches reflections
of birches and pines waver gently in the water,
and clouds—deep purple edged with gold—
lay themselves down and float.

Mercy Carter hurries toward her with a kettle and a rag.
They scoop up icy water and wash themselves
as best they can, and soon others join them.
Water cold enough to burn. But it feels good.

From further up shore a small group of men
scowls at them. The Indians stand thigh-deep in water,
very still, spears in their hands. Waiting
for the flash of fish. Fog coming in off the lake,
the men over there: for a moment it seems a dream vision

until Mercy flings a torrent of filthy water from the pot
and someone calls, and brush must be gathered
for a fire. That night they eat fish. Joanna licks
her fingers, wishing for more. They are all calm

and at least half-way content until Becca grips her arm.
What's that? What's that? A long, drawn-out wail
from the lake. A similar answer, ghosts
calling out, looking for something they've lost.
Then a warbled hooting, and more long notes.

Mournful. Lonely. *Loons,* the girls are told. *Birds
of the North. Spirits of the lake.* Something in Joanna
thrills to that eerie sound. Can a bird be a spirit?
No, Reverend Williams would say. *Certainly not!*

But he has taken a different route, and Joanna—
she finds herself beginning to believe it.

Between Sky and Water

If she weren't frightened of falling in, of drowning,
Joanna might be lulled to sleep by the watery swish

      of canoe paddles, and the thwishh of water leaping
      from the lake over sides of the boat.

She's wet and cold, wakeful, but the swaying
of the boat and rhythm of the paddles

      is a kind of lullaby. Becca's curled up
      dozing on furs that line the bottom of their boat.

She's in one of four big canoes made mostly of bark
their captors use for this part of the journey.

      It's lake and sky. Swirls of water where paddles dip.
      Breeze and the steady breathing of men

whose paddles push them through water,
through morning, into the afternoon. The shoreline

      slips by, clouds float overhead, everything moves
      to its own rhythm. The lake is high, Teka-ron-hioken says,

because of snow-melt. Thin silvery patches of ice
sweating in sunlight are busy changing from one form

      to another. They pass these by, and a floating log,
      and a big dark bird standing on a large rock, very still,

its wings outspread. Only when they get quite close
does it fly off. Joanna watches till it becomes a black speck.

      She imagines her own past winging away

like that bird, becoming smaller and smaller,
an image she sees behind closed eyes
after the real thing is gone.

Arrival at Kahnawake

The captives, a ragged bunch, mostly children,
are lined up near a pile of bundles. A stream
of villagers spills toward them, shouting
in their strange, exuberant language.
Dogs, snarly and yappy, race around
the legs of brown-skinned children.

Women chatter, gesture, and an old man,
entirely wrinkled, with beaded rings hanging
from his ears, a string of claws around his neck,
greets Teka-ron-hioken and the other Indians
just returned, then looks over the line
of captives, his eyes briefly meeting Joanna's.

> Ugly old man. He has no right to look at her.
> She wishes those claws around his neck
> were hers. She'd do some damage.

Louder than the barking dogs, louder
than the wind rushing through trees,
Joanna's heart is pounding.
If the others hear it, they'll think she's weak.
Her legs feel wobbly, her skin prickles.
She swipes at her nose that has started running.
It's the wind, the dust blowing around.

The returning Indians parcel out gifts—
all the things they've stolen
from homes they plundered.
An axe, a musket, a knife.

> She longs for a knife sharp enough
> to split an eyelash. To draw blood!
> A dagger! She'd never put it down.

A sewing basket, woven wicker, calico-lined,
that once belonged to the girls' mother
is handed away, and Becca cries out, steps
forward. Joanna yanks her back in line.

Two pewter cups. A medallion quilt.
Woolen shawl. Pistol. Cooking pots.

      Joanna feels empty as one of those pots.
      The wind has scoured her out. If she
      were a cooking pot, nothing
      could scrub away the scorch marks.

Joanna blinks, opens her eyes to the sight
of men showing off strings of scalps.
Becca's little friend Mehitable Nims—
those are her tight blond braids with a rusty rim
of dried flesh. When that little girl sang,
the birds stopped to listen.

      The savages are laughing.

First Night in the Longhouse

While men go off with their pipes and their talk, the sisters are taken to one of the long low houses covered with bark, smoky and dim inside, so many smells weaving together, and sounds: women talking in that other language—Mohawk—little boy laughing, dogs jostling by, sniff, snarl, yip, scratch, scratch.

Joanna peers through the smoke. Cooking pots simmer over fires. No windows, just holes in the roof. Her mind feels smoky— she shakes her head to clear it. All that anger, fear, energy dissolving into a heavy fog. The girls are folding into themselves, hardly able to stay upright. Women wash them, dress them in Indian clothes: deerskin leggings, loose tunics, and Joanna sheds her filthy rags without complaint.

Who are these women, what will happen now—they eat a good stew and their bodies say yes: meat, vegetables, grains—a nutty flavor, Joanna wants more, she wants to be back in her own home, she wants her mother and father but the food is good, how tired she is. Where is Father, where is Martin, someone took Joseph to a different longhouse, a black and white dog pushes its nose under her arm until a woman shouts at it, another woman combs her hair and braids it. Joanna just sits and lets whatever will happen, happen. The buzzing in her head slows down, her breath comes easier.

Dried apples hang from the rafters, clutches of corn, but no table anywhere, no chairs, just wooden benches, cooking smells, body smells, a woman humming or singing low. Sleeping areas closed on three sides face the fire, mats to lie down on and pelts, furs to wrap up in. Joanna does what she's told, she knows the meaning, if not the words, and crawls into a sleeping space. Becca follows and they let her. The girls' eyes sting from smoke, from weariness, what will happen next, what— they sleep, they sleep, they sleep.

Sweet Cradle of Sleep

Sleep. Joanna wants nothing but sleep.
To be cradled in the warm lap of sleep.
Filled with sweet blankness.
No memory, no knowledge, no need
to be brave. Just the warm embrace of sleep.

The past is a dream that's over now.
Her fears and her pains can go on without her.
The old life can turn to dust without her.
The future will unfold like new muslin cloth.
Blank, untouched, unknown.

The world needs no one's permission
to turn from day to night to day again.
Joanna is blind to the living; she's deaf.
She's nobody and the world is nothing to her.
Sleep. The only world she wants is sleep.

White Man in a Black Dress

Like a black sail crossing a dry sea, a large white man
comes slowly toward them, wearing a black dress.
A cross-shaped medal hangs on his chest.
None of the Indians take up their weapons.

Instead, they welcome him. They gather around.
A priest, a Catholic priest, Elizabeth Hull murmurs.
See, he comes from the mission on the hill.

      No wind today, but Joanna feels a tremble in the air,
      a purple vibration, everything unsteady.

She's with people who have killed her neighbors.
      They're treating her kindly.
The priest smiles.
      If you say the Catholic kind of prayers,
      Joanna knows, you end up in hell.

This man, this priest speaks the Indian tongue
and French, even English.

      Words, words—awful and unsayable.
      They buzz around her, blurring everything.

The priest writes names in a book. Names
of the captives. Joanna does not want
her name in a priest's book,
but maybe it will help someone find her?

      Could he rescue her?
      This papist. Priest.

Deerfield folk have called such ones French devils.
But he looks a little like her people.

No warpaint on his pockmarked face.
No scalps hang from his pasty-soft hands.

Quick and shallow,
Joanna's breaths rush in and out

but she gathers her courage, asks
Do you know where my father is, and my brother Martin?

He does not. But writes their names too.
Says he'll pray for them.

Wait, she chokes out her words.
These Indians, do you know what they did?
They crept into our village as we slept.
Burned our houses, hacked people to death.
My small brother...
I don't belong here.

Lifts her face up. Moisture gathers
in her eyes—she won't allow it to spill.

Deerfield again, blood bright on the snow.
Kahnawake, stew steaming in the pot.
Smoke in the air—here, there?

The Indian woman who acts like a mother
clucks her tongue, begins to pull on Joanna's arm.

Buzz, buzz. The air around her crackles.
Many eyes are on her—sharp as spears.

You are safe here, my child, the priest murmurs
just before he turns away.

Names

She will not call her *Nistenha*
for that means Mother. Joanna has a mother.
Or maybe not. But this woman isn't her.

Others call the woman *Red Leaf,* so Joanna
will call her that—or call her nothing at all.
She wants to hate her

for not being her real mother, but it's hard
to hate a woman with such kind eyes, a woman
who patiently mashes herbs into a soft grease,

works it into the sores on Joanna's feet,
into the cuts on her body.
Which are starting, now, to heal.

And the other woman wants Becca
to call *her* Nistenha, and Becca does,
though Joanna tells her not to.

*English—nah! t*he woman hisses at them
if they speak their own language. *Stands-in-Shadow*
is her name. She is *Teka-ron-hioken's* wife,

and *Red Leaf's* sister. And *his* name
means *Splits-the-Sky.* The scar on his cheek
looks different to Joanna now.

Like the signature of lightning.
Strange, he does not live with them
but comes in the night, and sometimes days.

Eats with them or with his mother, an old woman,
and then goes off with the men. He gives Becca

a little string of beads made from shells.
And Becca gives him a shy smile.
He has nothing for Joanna.
Their name for Becca is *Little Bird.*

They say she cheep-cheep-cheeps
from first light the way some small birds do.
Becca doesn't like it. But they are bird sisters now

for Joanna is *White Feather,* after the feather
she'd found on their journey,
a snowy owl's feather, which she kept,

touching the brown markings that stood out
against the white, sweeping it lightly
between her fingers. Her small treasure.

Silly—their new names. A girl is not a bird. Nor a feather.
Though she once met two sisters, back in her other life,
named Violet and Ivy. Names for plants, not people.

And she's known girls: Constance, Prudence, Mercy.
The qualities their parents hoped for
in their daughters? If Joanna had a girl child,

she'd name her Stands-Tall-in-Sunlight.
Or maybe Alice. Joanna is learning the names,
but she holds her English close.

No one can take that from her.

River of Stars

They wait inside the body a long time,
the tears that can't be shed.

They shine in odd places.
Row of dewdrops on a spider's web.

Beads of water flung to the sky
as river thunders over cataract.

A river carries water a long time
singing of stones and weather.
Then the falls. The release.

Sometimes the current of feeling
Joanna carries is too large,
too wild to name.

She steps out of the longhouse
to see why the black pup is howling.
Gathers it in her arms.

Looks up and sees beyond a sliver of moon
a river of glittering stars.

Through the long darkness
their light travels toward her,
listening to all she cannot say,

answering in spark and flash.

Words fall into her mouth,

wild bees looking for a hive.
Strange tickle—bzzzzt, bzzzzt.
But some feel good on her tongue.
Onen-hste—corn.
She hears herself say a word
she never knew she knew, and quick—
looks around, as if some other girl
had spoken. Some other *eksa-a.*

Brassy words, loud words
call out to her.   *Kahonk*—geese.
That one makes her laugh.
Already she loves it a little.
And words whisper to her.
Anowara—turtle. That quiet power.
Anowara, anowara.

When White Feather sleeps
words tumble into her dreams,
crooked stars falling from her new sky.
Katsi-tsa—moon.   *Tsiste-keri*—owl.
Without even thinking, she catches them.
Holds them.   *Nistenha*—mother.
And carries them with her into the day.

Wooden Spoons

Red Leaf is bent over a pair of moccasins,
working a row of white beads into the soft hide.

Rain creates its own curtain of beads,
but the longhouse is warm, almost cozy.

Splits-the-Sky is here, helping himself to something
from the pot. Stands-in-Shadow smiles at him.

Joanna is examining six wooden spoons.
She's learned that Red Leaf had a child once,

a daughter who died at a young age, and a husband
also, who carved these spoons. But he died too,

far from home. Splits-the-Sky swallows
and Joanna looks at the small round indentation

in the lower part of his throat—
shaped like the bowl of a small spoon.

She returns her gaze to the wooden spoons
that belong to Red Leaf. The handle of each one

has a head carved into it, each one slightly different—
this one with a beaky nose, that one with an open mouth.

Golden brown, the spoons are the color of maple syrup.
One spoon has a tiny crack. It's the one

Joanna likes the best. She slips the tip of her nail
into the slit. The carved face looks sideways at her.

Does Red Leaf look at these spoons and try to recall

the face of her lost husband?
Joanna squints, remembering her mother: green eyes,
tendril of wavy brown hair, a pair of busy hands.

She sighs quietly, replaces the spoons in the hanging bag
where they're kept. Red Leaf puts her hand

on the girl's head, briefly, gently. Outside the rain
is easing. It sounds like a heartbeat.

In the Word Home

In the word *home* she hears roam, hears a river's wild foaming.
The red door is no more.
Row of white trees and their darker cousins behind them.
A great horned owl hoots at the moon.

The red door is no more
and all of the names are changing.
A great horned owl hoots at the moon.
Many languages, bird and human, sing Joanna to sleep

but all of the names are changing.
Snow blows into her dreams, erases footprints.
Many languages, bird and human, sing as Joanna sleeps.
It is an honor to be part of the turtle clan.

Snow blows into her dreams, erases footprints.
Row of white trees and their darker cousins behind them.
It is an honor to be part of the turtle clan.
In the word *home* she hears roam, hears a river's wild foaming.

Instruction

Forget the spinning wheel. Forget
the heckling of flax. Forget the plank table
you scrubbed each day, the wood grain
glowing beneath your touch.

The youngest boy and what was done to him—
that you must forget.
Your mother's back as she ran into the trees,
holding her nightdress close. Forget, forget, forget.

And your father's shuffling silence,
his face blank, his eyes refusing
to see you anymore—
it's something to forget.
Here the men are bold.

And the women rule, open-hearted
in their laughter. They hold out their arms
to the young, carry their babies everywhere
strapped safely into cradle boards.

There is almost no crying.
There is no need for crying.

The old prayers you were warned never to forget
got lost on their way toward heaven.
Or fell to the frozen earth.

Words become smoke, promises turn to ash.
Forget all the old names, except your own.
Remember   Joanna.

You are not that girl anymore, but you carry her with you.
A person is made of skin and bones, hunger and hope,

footprints and many ghosts.
Hum quietly to your ghosts, Joanna.
Allow them to rest.

She Watches Her Brother

It's cool one day, warm the next
just like Joanna's feelings—
White Feather's feelings—

and her brother chases through the village
like a quick spring squall, appearing
and disappearing.

Yesterday's brief rain came hard and fast
leaving droplets behind that shone
as they dripped from new leaves.

She catches glimpses of Joseph—
that's not what they call him, though—
running in a pack with other boys, wrestling,

laughing, half-naked. His hair's a thick brown ruff
along the center of his skull, the sides shorn clean.
Streaks of mud cover his freckles.

He speaks Mohawk phrases full of vowels
and hard sounds, and when someone laughs or coughs
because he's said it wrong, he laughs too.

And tries again. Words in French
spill from him also—as if he just can't hold them in.
A priest, an occasional trader—he learns from them.

White Feather, as they call her, helps with the planting,
fetches water, and tries her hand at weaving splints
of softened ash wood into baskets. It's expected.

All this, while Joseph runs to the river, to the horse pen,
past the fields, through the woods—a half-wild boy.

The strictures he was raised with tossed away.
And the grief he's traveled through?
Has he left that behind too?
Does it sit on his chest when he hovers near sleep?

Maybe he'll kill it off with the bow he carries,
the notched arrows. He aims at rabbits,
at squirrels. Wants to go on a real hunt with the men.

They tell him he must learn patience first,
learn to start a fire with sticks, learn
to walk through the woods unnoticed,

learn to squat in one place for a long time, silent.
Silence, patience—these do not come easily
to the boy they call Spotted Colt.

But he can catch a bee in his fist,
where it hums and buzzes
until he opens his fingers, lets it go.

The Rapids

On her stomach beneath a curtain of willow leaves,
White Feather gazes toward the rapids

where the river rowdies to a noisy white froth.
Water rushes over and through this cascade,

no thought of danger. Sunlight falling toward it
breaks into a million glittering sparks—
becoming small flames that ride the water.

Kahnawake men know to portage their canoes
around this part of the river. Trappers and traders

hire them to do the same. But sometimes in a journey,
the rapids come on unexpected. She knows this.

You have to plunge through and hope to make it
past the boulders and the churning,
though you don't know up from down, water from air

or where this perilous ride will take you.

Seeing Sarah Burt

A hot wind kicks up dust and grit.
White Feather can hear corn stalks rattling.
        She helped plant them,
there among tree stumps, where squash
        spread out their green curling fingers,
their broad shady leaves, and beans grow too.
        All together, not in separate plots.

White Feather passes a group of boys
        playing the pass-the-bone game,
whooping and pointing, jostling one another,
        a blond-haired child among them—
could it be Billy Brooks? A pointy-eared dog
        is trotting along near the young man
known as Young Otter, who glances at her quickly

but says nothing as she walks
        toward a bend in the river.
It's a quiet place overhung with trees,
        her favorite spot to go for water.

Today a woman has waded in with her baby.
        She's swirling him through the cool
currents as he chortles and splashes.
        The woman looks up—it's Sarah Burt!

They speak English together
        though Red Leaf would disapprove.
English, like her old life, is best forgotten.
        The baby is Christopher.
He smacks the water with chubby hands.
        Little droplets catch the sun.

Sarah and her husband work for the black robes now.

They're not devil-worshippers.
They're just men, Sarah says, French men who speak
        to God in the Catholic way. Like men anywhere
they are kind one moment, thoughtless the next.
        Hungry. Worried. Sometimes ill. Just men.

Propped against a tree is a cradleboard.
        The women of the wolf clan,
who help Sarah with her baby, made it
        for the little one. Round flower designs
adorn the wood and it's filled with a soft lining
        of moss and cattail fluff.

These women, Sarah says, have been good to her.
        But Sarah and Ben do not want
to raise their son in Kahnawake.
        They hope to be ransomed.
To go back home.

Ransomed? Home?
        A hundred questions
storm White Feather's mind.

She holds her arms out for the baby.
        Dark hair frames his chubby face
and he blinks at her with the shiny brown eyes
        of a bear cub. Little Bear,
she wants to call him.
        Hello Christopher, she says instead.

He smiles at her and kicks his feet,
        reaches for her braid.
This is the only home he's known.

Her Sister Swimming

Becca—Little Bird, she's called now—has learned to swim.
White Feather watches the Kahnawake girls
Moonface, Twig and Gray Dawn

splash her, encourage her, laugh with her.
Tiny rainbows, as drops go flying.
Little Bird emerges from the river, sleek and smiling.

Stands-in-Shadow laughs at her almost-daughter
who's learned this new thing,
who's joined the other girls.

Stands-in-Shadow is so easy with the child.
Doesn't scold when Little Bird runs to her,
carelessly soaking her skirt.

Little Bird clutches moments of happiness,
greedy for them. The way she gulped down
mouthfuls of stew when they first arrived,

hunger the only sure thing.
White Feather should be glad for her little sister,
who can laugh again after all.

But a meanness rises up sometimes.
Bile in her throat. It chokes her
like smoke from wood that's green or damp.

Foolish girl! Sometimes White Feather wants
to shake her. *These people tore apart our lives!*
How do we forgive that?

White Feather presses her lips together,
says nothing. Her sister's cheeks have filled out again.

The purple shadows beneath her eyes are gone.
And today the cool breeze off the river feels delicious.
A gull shrieks, then repeats itself three times.
The girls in the river shout their fun, screech, shout again.

Now the gull hangs in the air
and White Feather, too, feels suspended
watching, listening. A little apart from all the rest.

She's suspicious of happiness, the way it sneaks up
unnoticed, the way it threatens sometimes
                              to carry her away too.

After Blackberry Picking

The others have turned back, but White Feather
goes a little farther, lingers a little longer.
Thin red scratches from the brambles mark her arms

and she's added new, itchy bumps to her skin—
gifts of the mosquitos—but she carries a basket
loaded with sweet berries. Beyond the brambles,

the far meadow smells of cedar and moss, dead leaves
and stone. In the patchwork of sunlight and shadow,
a movement. She stands very still and watches

a rafter of turkeys strut along, bobbing their heads,
the females crooning tuck tuck tuck
while two larger birds, males, gabble loudly.

They are the colors of old oak leaves
with bands of light and dark on their wing tips.
Almost beautiful but for their blue-bald heads

splotched red and warty, and the wattles.
They're pecking at the ground,
paying no attention to White Feather.

What is she to them? Tree shadow?
Weak, harmless thing unworthy of worry?
No. She is a stillness and they

are unanswered questions that cluck cluck cluck
near her feet, unseen by anyone.
If she told her brother or any of the men,

they'd see the birds differently.
They'd come with their bows and arrows

and bring back plenty of supper.
Hunger is the thing that drives everyone,
but there are many kinds of hunger.
Some kinds whisper. Others roar.

Now one turkey rushes toward her,
and it's become larger than the skinny bird
she'd seen moments ago.

White Feather shrinks back. They spread their wings.
Rush of air, flap flap and squawk. Commotion.
And they're gone. She picks up a feather,

fingers its delicate markings. Those birds
can fly away whenever they please
but they never do stray from their own kind.

The Circular Way of the World Reveals Itself

What kind of girl is she to lie under a tree
watching the sky, thinking thoughts that loop round
and round her mind, making her almost dizzy?

Yet no one clucks their tongues at her
or calls her *lazy child, foolish girl.*
They tell her stories instead.

Long ago, they say, the world was carried
on the back of a turtle.
Turtle Island—another name for earth.

The world is round, round as the shell of a turtle.
Time is sun and moon, the insect hum
of summer, fingers of winter, blue and stiff.
Time circles around and goes on forever.

Somewhere there's a girl who lives with her sister and brothers,
her mother and father. She doesn't fear Mohawks
because she's never seen one.
The girl dreams of whippoorwills and lightning bugs.

Somewhere there's a Mohawk girl
who lives with her family and her clan.
She doesn't fear whites because she's never seen one.
She dreams of a peaceful river—blue, green and silver.

When someone loses a loved one,
the Mohawks say: *His mind has fallen on the ground*
or *Her mind has tumbled down toward her feet*

because who can think straight
when the person you loved is suddenly gone?
Even your enemies have people who love them.

Sometimes White Feather forgets where she is,
who she is. Her mind walking backward loops around
to the days ahead, days that have no stories yet,

days that can only be imagined,
the way a wound imagines healing
into something strong.

Left Behind

Montreal! A crackle of excitement stirs
the air. Going to Montreal!
Beaver pelts, deerskins, baskets, corn
are loaded carefully into canoes.
They'll trade for supplies to last through winter.

They run back and forth, arranging things,
speaking briefly to those who will stay behind.
Spotted Colt is going! Red Leaf is going!
Splits-the-Sky is going too!

But White Feather and Little Bird are not.
Lump in the throat.
White Feather flexes her fingers, bites her cheek.
Little Bird hops up and down, gets in people's way,
asks questions. White Feather wants to know—
Why, oh why can't she go?

In her mind the city blossoms,
marvelous flower of many colors.
Ladies in elegant clothes. Shops and streets,
noise and glitter. Montreal!
It's not safe for you there, Red Leaf says.
Stay and help Stands-in-Shadow.
There are new hides to scrape.

Petals drop, turn brown.
Scraping hides.
With the jaw bone of a deer as her tool,
she'll need to clean away every last bit of flesh
from animal skins. For hours.
While her brother takes in the city!

A flicker of doubt nags her.

Will Red Leaf return? Will Spotted Colt?
Splits-the-Sky?

Long Neck, an older girl once called Elizabeth,
murmurs to her. *The Kahnawake worry*
you'll be recognized, or claimed, or taken away.
White Feather looks at her brother as he climbs
into a dugout. What about him?

But his dark hair is in the Mohawk style. His skin
is sun-browned. Blue tattoos mark his shoulders
and his neck. In deerskin leggings and moccasins,
who would see a Puritan boy?

The canoes shove off. A cormorant
that's been diving for fish wings away.
Little Bird sits on the ground,
tearing a brown leaf into shreds.
White Feather goes to the water and picks up
what's left—black feather floating there,
memory of a bird that's gone.

Visions, Divisions

White Feather sees her brother in church
where people bow their heads and pray on Sundays.
She tries not to look at the likeness of Christ
hanging on a wall, bloody and awful.

On other days, they pray to the Great Spirit,
Shonk-waiia-tih-son, protector of the world.
They thank the spirits of animals, trees,
and the good Mother Earth, who provides for them.

After church, White Feather and Spotted Colt talk.
He and the others have returned from Montreal,
everyone with new goods, new stories. Spotted Colt
has news of Martin—he's at a place called Sault-au-Recollet.
Tried to run away but was dragged back.

A wiry French trapper told Spotted Colt this and said
He's unhappy there, but you look quite the young savage!
And Spotted Colt did not know what to feel.

Insulted? Pleased?
Three Deer, his new father, is proud of him.
For he paddled till his arms ached,
carried goods, helped men of different tongues
speak to each other. French, English, Mohawk.

What do you think it really means, to be a savage?
White Feather asks. Spotted Colt picks up a smooth stone,
turns it over and over in his palm and thinks.

Bright flames leap against piles of snow—
their old village. Thick black smoke. Indians
hold scalps high, whooping victory shouts.
White men too, on other days, all grin and bluster,

trade scalps of dead Indians for pieces of silver.
Back in their Deerfield days, the cries
and bruised faces of a meek woman
and her young children, as others turned away.
What a man does in his own home is his business.

Spotted Colt blinks.
Throws the stone into a clump of weeds.
Don't know, he says, *but I like it here well enough.*

More Questions

White Feather seeks out her brother again
and finds him fastening arrowheads of chipped flint
to wooden shafts, his brow furrowed in concentration.
It's cold out, but Spotted Colt is sweating a little.

Come walk with me, she says.
        Not now.
Please. I want to ask you something.
He looks up at Three Deer, who sits beside him
near the entrance to a longhouse. The man nods.

About Martin, she begins, when they're away
from the others. *Do you think—
do you think he was trying to get away
so he could come and rescue us?*

Spotted Colt just looks at her. Then he says,
        I don't know. How would he know we are here?
What about Father, she continues. *Did you hear
any news of him?*
        No, no, I heard nothing of him.

*If he came for us—Martin, or even Father,
would you go with him? If you could, would you go?*
        Back to Deerfield, you mean?
Yes. Deerfield.
Spotted Colt shakes his head.
        No. There's nothing there for me.
Long pause.
        And you? If you had the chance, would you go back?

Deerfield. The old life.
A little whirl of snowflakes is finding them now.
A flake lands on her hand. She watches it
melt away.

64

Many People, They Lie Down

The sky is low and blank, waiting for snow.
What comes instead: urgent whispers of women.

Little Bird wants to find Moonface, wants to play,
but she is told *No! That girl and her family are sick.*
They carry bad spirits. A ridge appears
between Stands-in-Shadow's brows. Lines form
around her mouth. Nearby, some dogs snarl and snap.

Evil spirits can slip into the body of one who is weak.
But I am not weak, Little Bird says. *I am strong.*
She jumps up high three times on her strong young legs.

Many people, they lie down. Spots on the tongue.
Bodies on fire. *It's the pox,* Red Leaf says.
Tells how her grandmother died from it, years ago.
Tells of her uncle, surviving the pox—but seeing
no more than shadows in his remaining years.
Stands-in-Shadow nods. *It is so. It is so.*

Word comes—Spotted Colt is among the stricken.
He can barely croak out a word—sores in his mouth, his throat.
Little Bird and White Feather are kept away.
Evil spirits can slip into the body of one who is weak.

The fasting, the sweat lodge, the sachem
with his chants and rattles—nothing seems to help.
Many people, they lie down.
Spots on the tongue, sores on the skin. Bodies on fire.

White Feather sees one of the sick ones.
His skin like river mud that's bubbled and dried.
His awful, blistered face. His suffering.
Jesus on the cross could not have suffered more.

Is it wrong to think that?
Twelve people die.
Spotted Colt, they're told, could be next.

The fasting, the sweat lodge, the sachem
with his chants and rattles—nothing seems to help.
Spotted Colt—everyone's favorite.
He should not have to suffer so.

White Feather runs to the church and finds Father Bruyas.
His pockmarked face, blank and cold as the sky.
His black robe, his hands, soft and fleshy.

Furious words rush from her mouth.
You with your miracles, your holy water,
*cure my brother! Find a miracle for **him**!*

Day Filled with Chant

At first there are crows
perching on trees, strutting in fields
She hates the crows

their beady eyes, their
ack!
ack!
ack!
but an owl chases them all away

Spotted Colt lies in a small room
back of the church
where the scarred, homely kitchen girl
feeds him broth

White Feather wants to see him, but
no
no
no
she is forbidden

Two more have died
Spotted Colt might be next

When it's quiet, White Feather
can hear her own heart going
thud
thud
thud
in her chest.

She goes about her chores
whispering under her breath

Make him well
Make him well
Make him well

The notes of her prayer
become a small, brief cloud
in the cold air

to return later—
as snow

Snow and a Red Fox

For three nights snow fills her dreams.
It falls and falls.

Snow in her dreams and
in her world. Winter refuses to leave.
A red fox edges in, pauses on the threshold
of her night landscape—flare of red
against all that white.

Snow. Snow and a red fox looking on,
White Feather tells her mother.
Last night and the night before. And the night before that.
Shakes her head as if to clear it.

> *Night visions*, Red Leaf says.
> *A message from the spirit world.*
> *We'll go to Skywatcher.*

Skywatcher smells like smoke. His silver braids
are the color of smoke. He listens.
From the depths of many creases, Skywatcher's eyes
gaze at White Feather. Looks right into her mind.
She wants to turn away. Does not.

> *Your sorrow,* he says, *your worry*
> *will keep falling. Let Red Fox run through it.*
> *Red Fox—one of your spirit animals.*

That night—nothing.
But the next—Red Fox runs through falling snow.
A quick look back at her.
> As if to say—*Follow me.*

In the morning, they hear news.
Spotted Colt is better. The fever gone. He'll live.

What They Say After the Dying Has Ended

Evil spirits from the thorny ground,
from smoky air, from the powdery nests
of stinging insects, from witches or the evil eye—
they can enter the living body.

Some whisper: *small pox.*
Which means: *You Might Be Dying Soon.*

The days are short and dark and cold.
But the crescent moon has changed to full,
there behind its stream of clouds.
And the dying seems ended. For now.

Moonface lives, but not her mother.
Pale and thin, Spotted Colt lives.

His skin is dull and rutted. Some of the talking
has gone out of him. Yet he's become a story.
Father Bruyas gave him relics to hold
when the boy was blistered and burning.

Relics of Kateri, Lily of the Mohawks,
who survived the pox too.

A native girl, the priest said, *who knew miracles.*
But Joseph, you must promise to repent.
If you are to have a chance, you must accept the Catholic faith.
Spotted Colt— Joseph—would have promised anything.

Now he's a story. Father Bruyas likes to tell it.
Calls it *The Power of Faith*. Calls it *Miracle*.

The priest is proud. Moonface is angry.
She comes around crying.

No miracle offered to her mother.
And they were already Catholic.

Praying Indians...isn't that what outsiders call them?
What good did that do Moonface's mother?

Angry words. White Feather remembers
her own angry words. How she talked to the priest.
And she remembers her Red Fox. Not just a dream.
But says nothing.

Little Bird tells her friend, *That's all right.*
You can get another mother.

A Celebration

After long days away, the hunting party returns.
They carry much meat, much meat.
Tonight is for feasting.

Red Leaf braids White Feather's hair tightly,
fastens a clip with two white feathers into it,
holds the girl's head between her hands for a moment

looks into her eyes and smiles.
Carefully, Stands-in-Shadow paints tiny red dots
around Little Bird's wrists, many bracelets of red dots.

And the women get ready too.
Red Leaf puts on her quilled breast plate,
her new moccasins, and carries her feather fan.

Savory smells fill the air, meat cooking,
pumpkin and beans. People gather.
Speeches, too many speeches—the stomach talks louder.

Then the drumming, chanting,
drumming, dancing. Feet pounding the earth.
Men and women, old and young, feet pounding

drums beating, beating, beating,
men's voices rising and falling to the beat of the drums
while White Feather's feet tap, tap, tap.

Soon she is with the others, stepping forward,
stepping back, left, right, her feet
find the way as music enters her body,

beautiful people all around her, hair flying,
dancing, dancing, dancing,

their faces serious and joyous all at once.
Winter is hard, but they are strong.
The spirits are with them now.
They will not go hungry.

Without Goodbyes

She doesn't see John Sheldon or the small group
he's arrived with. She doesn't see Sarah Burt leave,
or Benjamin Burt, or their little curly-haired boy.
Ransomed, sold, gone back to the colonies.
White Feather doesn't get to say goodbye.

All day she and some other girls, along
with their mothers, wander far into meadows
near the hills, filling their baskets
with sweet wild strawberries. Some
of the women gather bark and roots
to be boiled as curative teas.

They're smeared with mud or bear grease
against gnats and black flies.
Twig wanders into the patch of leaves
that make the skin blister and itch,
but it's a fine day away from the village.
The ground smells good, the breeze is mild,
the sun warms them. Only a few berries
have been nibbled by birds.

An odd thing: most of the girls,
except for Twig and Following Spring,
knew each other before, back in their old lives,
when they were made to wear bonnets outside
to keep the sun from their pale skins.
Silly. After the long winter, the sun feels good.
It makes the skin glow.

They return to the village just as light
begins to fade. Legs aching from the long walk,
mouths and fingers stained red.
Flower bracelets on Little Bird's wrists

have wilted. Their baskets seep juice.
In the longhouse, women talk.
Men from the colonies have come and gone.
Some sort of French official was with them,
puffed up with his own importance.

Sarah and Ben and little Christopher—gone.
One of the men asked after She-Is-Planted,
a girl who was once called Eunice.
One of them shouted, making demands.
But She-Is-Planted was out in the meadow,
filling her basket along with the others.

Big Grandmother tells her family,
Her mother would never give her up!
Red Leaf and Stands-in-Shadow
pull their daughters close.
It makes my hair stand up! Red Leaf
says. *We would never, ever give up our girls!*
Isn't it so? she asks, and Stands-in-Shadow
nods as she picks a stray leaf
out of Little Bird's hair. *It is so. It is so.*

1710-1713

A Change in Seasons

Ree, ree, ree.
In a pond not far from the cornfield, spring peepers
greet a new moon with their high, thin music.
This is how spring comes.

Some say cold mud around the village
smells like life returning.
Some mark the maple ceremony,
sweet smell of sap boiling—start of a new year.

But for White Feather, it's the peepers.
Their wave of hopeful noise. Rhythmic cheeping,
a low grumbling vibration just beneath it.
Tiny frogs happy to be alive. As White Feather is.

When the village quiets on an evening
and that wave of reedy song drifts over her,
White Feather feels that sweet restlessness,
that yes, yes, yes. She is ready for spring.

Twilight is a purple cloak;
it feels beautiful on her shoulders.
Peepers call out their praise.
This is how spring comes.

Three Kinds of Religion

When White Feather was a white girl, a Puritan girl, religion was one man thundering warnings, urging watchfulness; it was devils and witches and wicked ways that can grab a person up if she's not careful. It was a single god, a frightening god, a male god. And it was reading scriptures, saying prayers, and obeying, always obeying the rules men say were spoke by God.

When she's in the mission church, religion is called Catholic, and it is people singing; it's light through the windows, and some words in a language called Latin. It's angels and a God who had a son who was also God and a ghost is in there somewhere. It's confessing bad thoughts and saying Hail Marys and looking at the cross so as to remember that suffering is goodness. But in White Feather's sinful heart, suffering is the opposite of goodness. There's some kind of holiness in this place, though. The miracle that saved her brother when he was near death, that happened in this church.

When she's in the woods, religion is the blackbird calling. It's sister trees, wild winds, little blue moths that skip over weeds down by the river. Each with their own spirit. What is prayer but thankfulness, for ancestors and animals, for morning sun. In this religion, spirit animals guide you. The singing comes from whippoorwills, from beetles clicking in tree bark and leaves rustling in wind. From the soft chatter of raindrops.

Young Otter

There's a little hitch in his stride.
White Feather looks for that
when she sees a figure emerging
from field or wood.

He's tall. His chipped front tooth—
she wants to press a fingertip against it.

When Young Otter walks beside her,
she feels the strength of his attention.
Not focused on her, but on every living thing
he sees or smells or hears.

He admires the deer
because they smell the rain before it arrives.

And blackbirds because they flash through the air
the way fish move in water,
suddenly swerving, all together.
Young Otter has a different way of knowing.

As his right hand lifts up and over
like a bird in flight, and his eyes
glance skyward, White Feather feels
a school of fish dart through her belly.

At night, he says, the raspy music
of grasshoppers steadies his heart.

She'll listen tonight.

Her Brother Goes on a Journey

A young man now, Spotted Colt is taller
than Three Deer, his father. He strides along,
talking in his new, lower voice. In French or English,
Mohawk or another native tongue.
And people listen when he speaks.

To the six Frenchmen he's leaving with,
he is *Joseph,* just as he is to Father Bruyas.
And White Feather hasn't forgotten Joseph,
the skinny, excitable boy he once was.

The men are loading birchbark canoes.
They'll trade and explore out west.
They've heard of a place called Great River—
they'll find it, Spotted Colt says, his eyes aglow.

In his rucksack are knives, rawhide, dried meat,
dried corn, extra moccasins, quills for writing,
notebooks, many supplies. He'll be gone a long time.
He has a job: Interpreter.

Cold Moon and Throws-Many-Stones say
he'd be better off hunting or raiding than going
to far shores with those white men.
A man should take care of his own. But Three Deer says
he brings honor to them all, and other men nod.
It is so. It is so.

White Feather hopes he won't get lost.
Or killed. Hopes he won't starve, won't forget
to return. He'll always be her brother,
though he's of the Wolf clan and she's of the Turtle.

Little Bird tugs on his sleeve as he's leaving

and demands of him, *Bring me back
something beautiful from far away, Spotted Colt.*
He just smiles. She's too old to be asking for gifts.

Bernadette, the woman who cooks for the priests,
the one who cared for Spotted Colt years ago
when he was near-dead with the small pox—
short, homely Bernadette—an orphan raised by nuns,

an unmarried woman with pockmarked skin
and frizzy hair that curls over her forehead—
she stands near the sisters and watches
Spotted Colt leave. Murmurs quietly to White Feather,
I hope he'll come back.

Encounter

The sinking sun leaves a red-gold swath of light
that ripples across the river. White Feather
slips into it, sheds the dust of the day.

The only sounds soft insect sounds
and the low thrum of a frog or two.
She turns on her back and watches clouds
turn deep violet, watches their edges turn gold.

All around her cool water. When she swims
toward shore, her hair flows behind her,
a soft swirl. Evening light fills her

as if she'd drunk it down; something else
fills her too, a longing for which she has no words.
She wrings out her hair, takes her skirt from the bush
where she'd slung it, swats lightly

at a cloud of gnats, and is startled
by a man stepping silently toward her: Cold Moon.
She knows of him, already a celebrated warrior.

Many scalps, many prizes. She's heard him laugh
only a few times, always a mocking laugh, never
the laughter of joy. He stares at her and reaches
for her wrist. Grips her, opens his mouth,

says nothing. His teeth very white. His grip strong.
Just then Black Dog rushes toward them,
a blur of noise and motion, barking, snarling.

Cold Moon drops her wrist and kicks at the dog.
A bark, a curse, a scuffle. A bird's sharp cry.
White Feather runs down the darkening path.

Brambles reach and sting, mark her with tiny trails of blood.
That night she feeds Black Dog by hand, then leans
against his thick body, an arm around the dog's neck.
Stop loving that smelly old dog, Little Bird tells her.

Big Grandmother laughs and looks toward Red Leaf.
Black Dog lies down and sighs, head on his paws.
White Feather says nothing.
Stirs the embers with a stick.

The Women Speak to White Feather

And they say soon, very soon, it will be time for White Feather to marry. The women of her clan agree and they have talked to the women of the Bear Clan and the Wolf Clan, who agree, for White Feather is no longer a child. The moon recognizes her womanhood and brings her the monthly bleeding, her skin is smooth and her hair has a luster that shows good health. When she marries there will be more meat for the family because it's a man's duty to provide—and Cold Moon is thought to be suitable. Gifts will arrive soon at the longhouse for White Feather and her mother to accept or not, and if they agree, the marriage will go forward. Cold Moon is strong and bold, and in need of a wife, his first wife and baby girl having died of fever, and his spirt is still restless with anger and hurt. He festers like a troublesome sore these several years later, but White Feather with her quiet, thoughtful ways may be a balm to him, and soothe his angers, and gentle him just enough so he can find his way to wisdom. That is the thinking. And after the marriage White Feather will be part of the group of young women, she'll have a man to tend, and before long she'll bring forth children with their merry ways and their needfulness. Her days will be full and useful. What more could one ask? Cold Moon is a strong man; he'll be a good protector. Already he is known as a fine warrior and hunter. Yes, it will be good. It will be good. But tears spring to White Feather's eyes and balance there, for he is not the one she wants.

Night Visions

Arrow flies through dusky air

Owl flaps off between trees
hooting, hooting

and someone is running—
a girl, her hair loose and tangled,
her breath ragged

Arrow, its point shining
ahh, the whistle of its flight

Red Fox—
fleeing, fleeing

harsh sound of someone
laughing, laughing

Owl drops a pale feather
into the moonlight

It twirls and floats
but does not land

Red Fox runs and runs
its tail a plume flowing behind it
like smoke

Flash of light, loud crack
of thunder—

White Feather startles awake
panting, panting

Resistance

Are you afraid to marry? asks Red Leaf.

> No answer. White Feather just lifts a finger
> to her lips and chews the nail.

My daughter. Something is wrong.
The shadows beneath your eyes—they come
from storm clouds in the spirit.

> White Feather watches a pair of squirrels
> chase each other over the ground, up a tree,
> their tails flicking. She shakes her head.
> *Afraid to marry? No, no, it's not that.*

Is it Cold Moon? You do not care for him?
If he seems fierce, that's just the man's pride
covering up his wounds. He needs
a woman. And he looks at you
in that certain way.

> White Feather sees in her mind
> something prowling through the woods,
> sees yellow eyes staring out from darkness.

Speak to me, daughter.

> Remembering Cold Moon's laugh, she hears
> the hyena, and her own voice becomes the loon
> warbling over the water, laughing or crying,
> it's hard to tell.   *Do I, do I*
> *have a choice in this?*

Red Leaf sighs. Surely her daughter
is old enough to marry. But this resistance,

this unhappiness…
The offerings will arrive soon.
You do not have to accept them.
But if you do not, we will lose honor.
You will be the girl who said no.

I want to do the right thing, I do. But…

She turns then, away from her mother.
If she must marry him, she will become
the darkness between stars.

Marriage Ceremony

After the blessing by the priests,
their names written side by side
in the big book, they go on
to the longhouse ceremony.
Most everyone's there.

The shuffling and chattering—it quiets down
as bride and groom seat themselves
on a bench in the center of the building,
his mother sitting near him, her mother
sitting near her. Little Bird admires
the wedding dress, made of soft, pale doeskin,
and decorated with fringe, feathers, beads.

Cold Moon looks serious, almost handsome.
A council chief gives the Marriage Speech.
Bride and groom nod, touch opposite ends
of the tribal wampum. They agree
to accept their marriage duties.

As the wampum belt is passed, guest to guest,
each one holds it briefly and offers
encouraging words or good advice
to the bride, to the groom. *Before you leave on a hunt,*
Cold Moon, give her your best arrow to keep
under her sleeping mats; it will keep her safe.
And *Cold Moon likes his corn cakes burned a little*
on the edges, soft in the middle.
When someone offers, *If you hear bears growling*
at night, never fear; the man's snores mean he's content,
the guests relax into smiles and laughter.

After sharing of the wedding cake,
dotted with nuts and berries, sweetened

with honey, the feather dance is performed.
Cold Moon leads the male dancers, while the bride
leads women and girls in the dance.
Drums pound, singers get louder, the speed
increases. Without once looking at Cold Moon,
White Feather waves her feather fan left, then right,
sways up and down, side to side, glad to repeat
the moves of Following Spring, the new bride.

Later, after a night of feasting and dancing,
as they prepare to leave with the others,
Little Bird sidles up to her sister,
and though she's been told not to speak of it,
she cocks her head at Cold Moon, whispers harshly,
He could have been yours!

Red Leaf Remembers

It was a long night of dancing, of celebration,
of bitter tastes in the throat,
of glances at her and away from her

but White Feather wakes up at dawn
to the chee-chee-chee, chee-chiree,
the whee whee, whistle-tweet of birdsong.

On another morning it might fill her
with sleepy contentment, but she sits up
in the blue-gray dark and wonders

what is wrong with those birds—
don't they ever think on winter coming,
don't they know they are made of nothing

but hollow bones and feathers?
Red Leaf stirs and tells White Feather to get up,
to walk with her to gather kindling,

their supply is low. As they walk, Red Leaf talks.
After her husband had been dead for two years,
and her little daughter for one, another man

came offering marriage, and she considered it.
Considered it. Her mind a whirling wind.
She went to the hills and sat for many hours

thinking of the reasons it would be good.
But that man (she does not name him) had a certain smell
that made her body lean away when he was near,

and his voice, when he spoke, was thick and moist.
She kept remembering Standing Elk, the way he moved

toward her and away, the stories he'd told in winter
his voice a low music as he worked on his carvings.
She kept remembering, and her heart said no,
she could not marry this other one. And she did not.

Red Leaf pauses for a moment, looks off into some
unseeable distance, and continues, *Sometimes, without
a husband or a child, I felt like nothing. The wind*

*might blow me away. But there were other women
to sigh with and laugh with. And then you came,
White Feather, and Little Bird too. And every breath*

I took was the world, filling me. White Feather
risks a glance at this woman who has her own
surprising life of loves and doubts and secrets,

as Red Leaf continues talking. *Cold Moon—maybe
he was not the right one for you. Do not worry, daughter.
You still have time to make a good marriage.*

White Feather's head hurts, but a door in her heart
has opened. She lifts her eyes from her feet
and meets her mother's gaze. The sun has fully risen.

Now let us fill our baskets with sticks, Red Leaf says briskly,
*and get back to rouse your lazy sister. We'll make
the corncakes extra sweet this morning.*

On a Day Full of Summer

White Feather steps out of the field
with a basketful of ripe squash
near to overflowing

an arrow of geese honks by overhead

Following Spring steps through late summer heat
one hand gently rubbing her midsection,
in a circular motion

and glances at White Feather, smiling a secret smile

in the fields, bees are humming
and little boys run toward the river path,
happiness trailing them

Black Dog's gone off to pant in the shade

long ago White Feather stepped out
of one life, into this one
the way startled geese step toward the river, settle and glide

she wonders, *how do they find their way?*

Cloud Woman

White Feather and her friend, Makes-the-Grass-Wave,
are fetching water. The dew has not yet dried,

it beads the spider webs they pass, catching
early morning light. White Feather glimpses a fox

trotting along the tree line, its tail a russet plume
tipped in black. In a blink it vanishes, but she smiles.

It's a good day when one of her spirit animals appears.
Her other guide, Owl, calls to her some evenings,

thrumming a deep *hoo-hoo,* its voice full of forest and sky.
But what is that noise coming from the bramble canes?

It's coming from over there, her friend tells her.
They creep closer, where something is moving.

It's an old woman, crouching close to the ground,
crying a little, moaning. It's Cloud Woman,

grandmother, no—*great* grandmother—of Young Otter.
They set the water jars down, help the old woman up,

brush dirt from her, pull off some prickly burrs.
Cloud Woman can't tell them what's happened. She mumbles

something about the East Wind, something about twins.
She peers around, shreds bark from a stick, coughs.

I'll help her home, White Feather says,
and I'll come back later for my water.

Makes-the-Grass-Wave says she will take her own water

to her mother and tell the others what's happened.
White Feather puts her arm around the old woman's back
and guides her forward.

As they near the longhouses, Young Otter
hurries toward them. *Great Grandmother!*

The woman raises her gnarled hand,
color and texture of an old oak leaf,

and touches the young man's cheek.
Looks blearily into his eyes. *I think I know you,*

she mutters. *You're the good twin.*
and *I didn't mean to, I didn't know...*

He murmurs kindnesses to her and, with White Feather,
guides her along toward home.

Thank you for this, he tells White Feather. *Her spirit—*
it has been wandering these days, and she tries...

she tries to follow it. Two women hurry toward them,
Young Otter's aunt and grandmother.

They take Cloud Woman in, patting her, soothing her,
and they nod at White Feather.

Young Otter says he'll go with White Feather
to get the water she's left behind, but she protests,

You don't need to, Young Otter. I can get it.
He just smiles and walks on with her.

A Hundred Men on the Field

Amid odors of wood smoke and tobacco, two groups of hunter-warriors prepare. They'll leave soon for many days. But now they gather round a fire, sprinkle it with tobacco. Smoke rises toward the sky gods. A long, long field's been cleared for the contest. Young Otter, who usually walks calm and easy from place to place, has been taking long runs day after day so he'll be ready. Splits-the-Sky has fasted and prayed to his spirit animals for strength, for patience, agility. It's the same kind of strength and endurance they'll need on the hunt. But now, the game is to begin.

The men carry long, curved game-sticks of hickory wood. Splits-the-Sky has the head of a hawk carved into the handle of his. Strips of deer hide make a net on the end of each man's stick. There's a ball made of deer hide too. The game is called *tewaarathon*. Visiting traders call it *lacrosse*. Men are on the field, two large groups facing each other. A muttering in the crowd, excitement, like a wind rustling through trees before a storm. The signal is given. A shout, *yah!* Swarms of men go after the ball. At the two far ends of the long field are pairs of trees. To fling the ball between the trees, they run and shove, they swing their sticks, they shout and grunt. Over a hundred men swarm back and forth. All those bodies—it's hard to see the ball.

Dust and noise. A dog's sharp cry and string of yelps as it runs off crying; smacked by a stick. Black Dog paces the sidelines, barking, barking. Women, children, old men shout encouragement. Pounding feet. A medicine man helps the injured. Traders wager on which side will win, which players will prove the strongest, the fastest. A little boy runs up and down the edge of the field; his mother pulls him back. When the ball lands between the feet of a man named Dragging Canoe, Cold Moon goes after it, but can't get it. He whacks his opponent with his stick, and the ball leaps away. Dragging Canoe limps off the field, his lips stretched wide in pain or fury, his teeth showing. Blood runs down his leg from an ugly gash.

Exciting at first, the game begins to seem endless. The men run, grunt, shove, wrestle, fight, scream, swing their sticks. Sun is low when the game ends. Cold Moon's team has won. Following Spring goes to her husband, full of smiles. Stands-in-Shadow offers water to Splits-the-Sky, who gulps it down. He takes more and splashes it on his face. He persisted through the entire game, but limps now, covered in sweat, exhausted. White Feather finds Young Otter worrying over a crack in his stick. When he sees her, he smiles. She tells him she was watching when he hit the ball through the trees. *Such shouting when you did that,* she tells him. His smile widens. There will be feasting tonight. All will be praised for their strength, their courage. Prayers will be offered for the hunt to come. She must go, and help prepare the food. *I'm very hungry,* Young Otter admits, touching her fingers with his just before they part.

They Marry

White Feather and Young Otter

because he sees things with his mind, his heart
    because she listens with her eyes wide open
because his slow smile shows a chipped tooth
    because her eyes are flecked with gold, ponds in sunlight
because some days he smells like the forest, other days he's smoke
    because on days full of rain, her hair smells like stones
because when he's away, her losses gather in a huge black wave
    because fireflies come to him in a dream, a necklace for her
because once they sat still together,
    watching cloud shadows move over a meadow

Together

Not for them, the longhouse on their first nights of marriage,
so White Feather and Young Otter travel by canoe,

around the bend in the river, heading north and east,
passing boulders and islands, water birds and beaver.

They spot a moose with her two calves up to their knees
in water, the stems of plants spilling from their mouths.

Young Otter is a skilled hunter,
but he will not kill these creatures—the young

need their mother—they need time to grow up.
White Feather watches Young Otter take the first taste

of the fish she has cooked. He smacks his lips,
then takes a piece and puts it to her mouth.

They feed one another until they are greasy and laughing.
The campfire burns low, but still sends sparks spiraling upward,

and they watch, lying together on a buffalo robe.
Young Otter caresses her cheek, her neck, and she

leans into him. He kindles her and they become the fire.
All night as they doze and wake, reach out toward each other,

and sleep, sharp stars tremble overhead.
An owl calls. White Feather stirs, breathes in

the musky smell of him and the spicy cool
scent of pine needles. A halo surrounds the moon.

A Journey Is a Story, Is a Circle Like the Moon

The strawberry moon is high and round
when Spotted Colt comes back,
his pack bulging with gifts, his notebooks
full of drawings. His arms and legs
have become the muscular limbs of a full-grown man
and his head is full of words, full of stories
that spill out when he smokes with other men,
renewing his ties.

When he learns White Feather has married,
he is surprised and then not surprised.
He sits with Young Otter, talking about Chigagou,
where travelers portage their canoes
between great lakes and a great river.

And he talks of a river called Maushomine—
some call it Illinois—and the geese, cranes,
ducks, and swans that fly up all at once
in an uproar of wings. Pike and trout plentiful,
and sturgeon longer than a man is tall.

He talks of buffalo thunder, the sound
made by thousands of buffalo, and the storm clouds
of dust they kick up. Tells of their great
sorrowful faces, as if dreams of some sad fate
follow them everywhere, never letting go.

He talks of fruit trees with sour apples
and sweet plums, of walnut trees heavy
with nuts, of a French village where they make
wine, a drink that is red and rough-tasting
but good. Quite good.

He sleeps and eats and talks and talks.

He gives Little Bird a small bag of soft hide
delicately beaded and fringed.
Her eyes shine. She runs off to show Moonface.
And to White Feather he gives
a most curious gift, a snail turned to stone.

Says he believes it's older than old, that the mud
it moved through turned slowly to rock.
White Feather traces ridges in the stone,
circular, like seasons, like years, a stone snail
round as the moon that hovers cold and bright
just beyond the treetops.

Stone snail, traveler with its own story,
one she'd like to know. A small creature—
It had its little life, but never quite let go.

Another Story Begins

When the wind throws dust in the air and a sudden
storm sweeps into the day, when sheets of rain
rush sideways, blinding and cold, you submit
to the power and beauty of it, a little afraid.

When her belly tightens like a drum, softens a little,
tightens again, and waves of pain clench
at her harder and harder, she pants and she paces,
till her shuddering body sways and she groans an animal sound.

Red Leaf puts her arms around her, supporting
her daughter. Little Bird gives her sips of broth.
Near the end, Stands-in-Shadow gives her a clean, hard stick
to bite on, so she will not cry out, will not give birth to a coward.

Terrible pressure, and then great relief. Owirá-a! The baby!
A boy: dark thatch of hair, purplish skin. Silence—it feels long.

The space between lightning and thunder
is breathless when a storm is closing in.
Inhalation, long pause filled with waiting.
This moment—right after the birth—feels like that.

Outside, a dog barks sharply. Then they hear a whimper, a cry,
louder. An indignant wail! And the infant turns rosy.

It's all a confusion of busy hands and women's low voices.
White Feather is pushed and pulled and cleaned. She's given
water, and finally, finally handed her son. He stares at her
with dark gray eyes, his mouth forming a perfect O.

Young Otter returns with his hunting party and barges in
like a gust of wind. Red Leaf stops him, orders him to wash
before he can touch his woman or his new child. Yes, yes.

He obeys. Shakes water from his skin, goes to White Feather.
He brushes a strand of hair from her forehead.
Young Otter leans toward her, and she smells the woods
on him, faint odors of moss and musk. He turns to the baby.
Grins as the little one grips his finger. A good strong grip.

Epilogue

There is some information available regarding the lives of Deerfield residents who survived the attack in 1704. However, there is little information on the Mohawks living at Kahnawake at that time. Here is what happened to some of the individuals mentioned in the book.

<u>Martin Kellogg Sr.</u> was ransomed in 1706 and returned to Massachusetts. He relocated to Suffield, Connecticut. His wife, <u>Sarah Dickinson Lane Kellogg</u> escaped from the house during the raid in 1704.

<u>Anna Kellogg Severance</u>, daughter of Martin and his first wife, Anna Hinsdale, was living elsewhere at the time of the raid. Several years after the raid, she and her husband bought what remained of the Kellogg home from her father.

<u>Martin Kellogg Jr.</u> escaped from captivity with three other captive teens in 1705, but was recaptured in 1708. He was ransomed in 1712. Later, he joined a small group that travelled to the Montreal area attempting to negotiate the release of other captives. This effort was partially successful. He persuaded his brother Joseph, then a young adult, to leave Kahnawake and return to the colonies. At one time, Martin managed a boarding school for Native American boys, although many of his boarders left, complaining of ill-treatment.

<u>Joseph Kellogg</u> is credited with being the first English settler to see the Mississippi valley. Later he provided information that helped correct maps of that area. Joseph became a fur trader and interpreter in New France and eventually returned, somewhat reluctantly, to the colonies, persuaded to do so by his half-brother Martin. He became a captain in the army and an interpreter. Eventually Joseph Kellogg became Commander at Fort Drummer. He married Rachel Devotion and they had five children.

<u>Joanna Kellogg</u> lived and married in Kahnawake. Some reports indicate

that her Mohawk husband became a chief. She, several of her children, and possibly her husband visited Martin Jr. in Newington, Connecticut at some point, but she could not be persuaded to enter the house or to extend her visit for long. Considerably later in life, most likely after the death of her husband, she remarried and moved to an area in Pennsylvania that was then "Indian Territory," but gradually opened to white settlement. By that time her children were grown or nearly grown and were probably living among the Mohawks at Kahnawake.

Rebecca Kellogg lived at Kahnawake for well over 20 years. Eventually she returned to New England, where she remarried at the age of 50, to Benjamin Ashley, who was hired to work at the "Indian School" that Martin Kellogg Jr. had opened. She worked there as an interpreter. Even after returning to New England, she identified as a Mohawk. She died in 1757 at the Iroquois village of Ouaquaga, where she was given the name Wausaunia, which means "the bridge." She was a strong woman able to bridge two cultures.

Benjamin and Sarah Burt were ransomed, along with their son Christopher, in 1706. They travelled down the St. Lawrence river, and then by sea to Boston. Sarah gave birth to a second son (named Seaborn) during this journey.

Reverend John Williams, once he was released from captivity in 1706, wrote and talked about the raid and its aftermath. His children Samuel, Esther, and Warham were also captured during the raid and held near Montreal until they were released with their father. His son Stephen, who was nine at the time of capture, stayed with some Abenaki Indians for over a year, but was eventually ransomed and sent to join his father. Reverend Williams made several attempts to negotiate the release of his daughter Eunice, but was unable to do so. The child's Mohawk family loved her, and she had no interest in returning to her former life.

Eunice Williams stayed in the Kahnawake community, married there, and raised a family.

Father Jacque Bruyas died at Kahnawake in 1712. Some sources say that he left behind a grammar of the Mohawk language and a catechism and prayer book in Mohawk, although it is generally thought that there was no written form of the Mohawk language at that time.

Kahnawake, sometimes spelled Caughnawaga, is one of several Mohawk First Nation territories found in Canada. It was settled as a Jesuit mission, and the Jesuit Mission Church of St. Francis Xavier still stands within the community. The name of this settlement comes from the Mohawk work kahnawà:ke, which means "place of the rapids." It was a matrilineal society. When a couple married, they lived with the woman's family. Although chiefs were men (three from each of the three clans, making a total of nine), it was women who selected the chiefs.

In the twentieth century, many men from Kahnawake found work as iron and steelworkers in Canada. Thirty-three Kahnawake Mohawk men died in 1907 when the Quebec bridge collapsed, a terrible disaster for the community. Many others went to New York City and worked on skyscrapers and bridges.

Many community members have ancestry that is multi-racial, as there was intermarriage between the Native peoples, French colonial troops, and nearby shopkeepers, as well with captives who stayed in the community. Although people of European descent were among those long-welcomed into the community, concern has developed about preserving cultural identity. In the 1980s, Kahnawake enacted a law to restrict residency to Mohawk natives.

About the Author

Ginny Lowe Connors, a retired English teacher, is the author of several poetry collections. These include *Toward the Hanging Tree: Poems of Salem Village* (Antrim House, 2017), as well as *The Unparalleled Beauty of a Crooked Line* and *Barbarians in the Kitchen*. Her chapbook, *Under the Porch,* won the Sunken Garden Poetry Prize, and she has earned numerous awards for individual poems. Connors has also edited a number of poetry anthologies, including *Forgotten Women: A Tribute in Poetry*. Connors holds an MFA in poetry from Vermont College of Fine Arts. She is a former poet laureate of her hometown, West Hartford, Connecticut. She runs a small press, Grayson Books. A Board Member of the Connecticut Poetry Society, she is co-editor of *Connecticut River Review*. Connors writes a column for the *Hartford Courant*: "CT Poets' Corner."

Made in United States
North Haven, CT
03 March 2022

16721889R00071